HEART AN

THROUGH THE EYES OF MARK

Ian Paul

The Bible Reading Fellowship
OPENING THE BIBLE

Contents

To Elizabeth Ruth
(born 24th July 1996)

May you too learn to see
through the eyes of Mark,
and so doing grow to love
the Lord Jesus with all
your heart and mind and
soul and strength.

Introduction

Mark's Gospel is, at sixteen chapters, the shortest of the four we have in the New Testament. It has fairly simple vocabulary (and so is often the first studied in courses in New Testament Greek!) and is frequently (wrongly, in my view) regarded as having the least sophisticated theology.

How does Mark relate to the other Gospels?

Until recently, it was thought that Mark simplified and abbreviated Matthew's Gospel, thought to be the earliest, and was therefore seen as somewhat 'second-rate'. However, in the nineteenth century much thinking was done about the way oral traditions come to be written down, and as a result many people came to view Mark's Gospel as the earliest, with Matthew and Luke copying parts of his material. The majority view now is that Mark was written first. Interestingly, Mark is the only one to call his account of Jesus' life a 'Gospel' (Mark 1:1).

Mark was thoroughly overshadowed by interest in Matthew in the early centuries of the Church's history. In the fourth century, St Augustine called Mark a 'foot-follower and abbreviater of Matthew', and in the late fifth century, Victor of Antioch complained of a complete absence of commentaries on Mark.

In a number of the stories in both Matthew and Mark, Matthew's version appears to be more impressive and dramatic. So, Jesus heals two demoniacs, not one (Matthew 8:28; Mark 5:2); Jairus' daughter is dead already, rather than at the point of death (Matthew 9:18; Mark 5:23); the cursed fig tree withers instantly, rather than the next day (Matthew 21:19; Mark 11:14, 20)—and so on. But at the same time, these stories in Mark include details that Matthew does not. Thus, only in Mark do we hear how the demoniac has been restrained (Mark 5:4–5). Only in Mark does Jesus silence the mourners at Jairus' house before turning them out (Mark 5:39). Only from Mark do we know how the woman with an issue of blood has spent all her money on doctors' fees (Mark 5:26).

As a result, whilst the miracles in Matthew sound dramatic and impressive, Mark's accounts are more simple and direct—it is a very 'human' Gospel. And it makes it difficult to believe that Mark has simply abbreviated Matthew.

Several of Mark's stories have complicated structures, with one story being 'dovetailed' into another. For example, only Mark places the accusation that Jesus is possessed within the story of his family thinking he is mad and coming to find him (Mark 3:19–35). In the same way, Mark places the cleansing of the temple within the incident of the cursing of the fig tree (Mark 11:12–25)—and he does a similar thing with five other pairs of stories. In these two examples, and elsewhere, Matthew 'unpicks' the stories, and presents them separately. This suggests that, in terms of arrangement of material, Matthew is simplifying Mark, rather than the other way around—which suggests that Mark is the earlier Gospel.

Who wrote this Gospel?

The author is probably John Mark, who accompanied Barnabas and Paul on part of their missionary journeys (see Acts 12:12 and 12:25—13:13). An early tradition (Papias, writing in the second century, quoted by Eusebius, writing in the fourth) says that Mark was Peter's *amanuensis*, or secretary, so that what we have is, essentially, Peter's testimony about Jesus' life. However, Papias notes that Mark did not write these things down 'in order', that is, in chronological order. We should pay attention to the order of events to understand Mark's perspective, rather than to work out the chronology of Jesus' life.

Mark includes some unique eyewitness details in his stories—several of which are mentioned above. My favourite is that only Mark mentions that the grass was green at the feeding of the five thousand (Mark 6:39)—not without significance, when you realize that the heat of the Palestinian summer turns the grass brown by July. Mark is also the only Gospel writer to record the healing of a blind man at Bethsaida (Mark 8:22–26). The elements of the story are difficult to make sense of, other than as details noted by an eyewitness.

At some places, Mark seems to be gathering material together in order to provide a 'bird's eye' view of Jesus' ministry. Thus in the section after the introduction, we are given a specimen day—a 'day in the life' of Jesus—to show the sort of things he was doing in the Galilean ministry (Mark 1:21–34). At other points, similar material is gathered together. This is most obvious perhaps in the teaching section in chapter 4. In the 'dovetailed' stories mentioned above, Mark seems to be saying that we must understand different incidents in the light of each other—the cleansing of the temple needs to be understood in the light of the withered fig-tree, and vice versa.

When was it written?

Mark's Gospel was probably written around the year AD65, just after Paul's letters, but before the devastatingly important destruction of the temple in AD70. There does not appear to be quite the same significance attached to Jesus' conflict with 'the Jews' as in, say, Matthew or John. The first readers of Mark were probably a mixture of Jewish Christians in the *diaspora* (Jews living away from Palestine, and much influenced by Greek culture and ideas) and Gentile converts to Christianity. The Gospel may have originated in Rome, though the author seems to be familiar with the way of life of ordinary Palestinians.

Mark alone adds the editorial comment '(thus he declared all foods clean)' in 7:19, which suggests that his audience was a mixture of Jewish and Gentile Christians.

He also uses a number of Latin terms, which supports the theory that he wrote for a Roman audience. At two points, he explains Greek terms in Latin: 'two *lepta* [Greek] which make a *quadrans* [Latin]' (12:42); and 'the palace, that is, the *praetorium*' (15:16). The first of these explanatory notes is particularly

4

telling, since the *quadrans* was not in circulation in the eastern part of the empire, but only in the West. Mark is the only Gospel to include Jesus' saying, 'Everyone will be salted by fire' (9:49), which would have had particular relevance to Roman Christians persecuted under Nero. And it is striking that the climax of the Gospel is the declaration of Jesus' identity as Son of God by the centurion at the cross. This declaration echoes Peter's in chapter 8 that Jesus is the Christ, and together these fulfil the 'promise' of the prologue that this is 'the gospel of Jesus Christ, the *Son of God*' (1:1).

Overview of the studies

It is not possible to cover every verse of Mark's Gospel in this number of studies. However, the way Mark has arranged his Gospel gives us some help. He often gathers together material that illustrates a theme, so by looking at one of these sections we can gain a fresh insight into that theme in the Gospel as a whole. For example, whilst Jesus is presented as a teacher throughout the Gospel, there is a concentration on his teaching in chapter 4. By looking at this section on teaching, we can understand Mark's overall perspective on Jesus as teacher.

The eleven studies are as follows:

* 1. Mark 1:1–15	'The beginning of the gospel…'	The 'prologue' to the Gospel, introducing its main themes
2. Mark 1:21–45	'All who were sick…'	Jesus' ministry of healing, and the impact it has in Galilee
3. Mark 2	'Old cloth and new…'	The conflict that Jesus' ministry provokes
4. Mark 4:1–25	'He began to teach them…'	Jesus' teaching ministry, and the secret of understanding it
5. Mark 5	In action against hostile forces	Jesus' power over the spiritual opposition to his ministry
6. Mark 6:30–52	'Utterly astounded…'	Jesus' miracles and their meaning
* 7. Mark 8:27—9:13	The crucial question	The turning point: the recognition of Jesus' identity
8. Mark 11:1–25	'The Lord will come to his temple…'	Jesus arrives in Jerusalem, with both blessing and judgment
* 9. Mark 14:12–31	The Passover supper	The last stage of preparation in the Passion narrative
* 10. Mark 15:1–39	The crucifixion	The climax of the story—and of the whole Gospel
* 11. Mark 16:1–8	The resurrection	The unfinished ending—what happens next?

You may want to spend fewer than eleven sessions studying Mark. In that case, choose the studies that most interest you and will be of most relevance to your group—though you would do well to include the five that are asterisked.

Reading the Gospels

In the Gospels we have a record of events in Jesus' life, death and resurrection from four different perspectives. We can treat this fact in one of two ways: either we can use the different accounts as part of a jigsaw puzzle, and try to put them together into one picture, the 'true' picture of Jesus' life; or we can look at the individual views, and try to understand what is distinctive about each of them. The first way essentially concentrates on findings similarities between the accounts; the second focuses much more on the differences, or rather, the distinctives.

Many Christians over the years have used the first approach, but it has a number of drawbacks. In the first place, the Gospels seem to have differences that do not fit together well, such as the story of the healing of the blind man outside Jericho. This need not ultimately be a serious problem, and need not undermine our confidence in the Gospels as eyewitness accounts. But we can use up an awful lot of energy working out these harmonies, and often they do not necessarily help us to *understand* the Gospels any better.

Secondly, it is not clear that this is what we are meant to do with the Gospels. Did each writer only give us a partial account, as only one piece in a jigsaw that on its own was, at best, incomplete and, at worst, useless? It certainly appears that the early Christian communities valued each of these different Gospels.

Thirdly, we need to think about how we believe God speaks to us. The Gospels are testimony to the events they record, but they also interpret them. It is the events, rightly interpreted by scripture, that are important. (This is, in fact, true of all events; they are always presented to us with some kind of interpretation, even if this is the interpretation we give to them as we witness them. Otherwise we would not be able to make sense of them.) Therefore, we must take the interpretation of the events as seriously as the events themselves.

So when we read the Gospels, it is often instructive to compare one Gospel with another, not to find out what is missing from, in this case, Mark, but to see what is really there—to discover Mark's own unique perspective, and how he wants us to understand the story of the life of Jesus.

If you would like to study the first three Gospels in detail, and see how they compare, you might want to buy a 'synopsis'. This is a version of the Gospels where parallel passages are set out side by side, making it easy to see similarities and differences.

Leading a group

Purpose

Before you even meet, it is worth asking the question, 'What is this group for?' Hopefully, the first answer to this will be, 'To read the Bible and learn together to grow in our discipleship.' But not every member of your group will have the same expectations. For some, the highlight of the time together will be the coffee and chat with people who grow to be friends. So keep an ear open to expectations, and let that shape the way you meet. This might include coffee (before or after), perhaps a time of worship, the study, prayer. Priorities may change as you grow together. One important area of expectation will relate to time. A great study can be spoiled by finishing late, with everyone tired out. So make a point of trying to finish on time—without cutting off discussion in mid-flow! (If there is a clock in the room, sit opposite it, and you can keep an eye on the time without continually looking at your watch.)

Preparation

It is important that you, or whoever is leading the study, prepares adequately. The purpose of this is not so that you know the answers, but so that you can guide the group through the study effectively. You cannot navigate if you are not familiar with the map! This will mean reading the introduction to the whole study, reading the passage, looking up the leaders' notes, and then working through the questions yourself. Some of the studies are quite full, and you may not want to tackle every question. You must judge what is going to be most appropriate with your group. Do pray for the members of your group weekly.

Setting

Most groups are served best by meeting in a home, where people can relax. Groups usually function best when everyone is sitting at the same level, though this is by no means essential.

Reading

In general, it is usually worth breaking a passage up into manageable chunks, even if you read it all at once. Interest is retained by means of a change of voice. (In a visual age, many are unused simply to *listening*.) However, I think it almost always worth avoiding 'reading around', where each person reads a couple of verses. Apart from potentially embarrassing someone who is uncomfortable reading aloud, the arbitrary change of reader never does justice to the structure or rhythm of the passage, and so makes listening more difficult. And then there is a constant change of translation...

Bible versions

If most people in your group have the same translation, try and stick with that one—and be thankful! There are many English translations around nowadays, but they are not all equally good for study. If possible, encourage group members to bring a more literal version (amongst the ones they possess), such as the RSV, NRSV or NIV, rather than more colloquial, idiomatic translations, such as the Living Bible, or the Good News. Try and avoid the AV ('King James') if you can—it is so difficult for most people to understand (and contains a number of mistakes!) that it can slow down comprehension and the whole study. But all this needs to be handled sensitively; people get very attached to the version that they have been reading over many years.

Questions

In general, do allow the members of your group to think out answers for them-selves—even to struggle a little—as part of the exercise is to help the group to learn how to ask (and answer) questions about scripture. We are not just giving them fish, but teaching them to fish too—not just feeding them, but helping them to feed themselves. This means that you need only mention the back-ground information as and when it becomes appropriate during the process of answering the question, perhaps as a stimulus, perhaps to answer someone's question of information.

You will find that the questions given tend to follow the form:

- *Discovery: What is the passage actually saying?*

- *Understanding: What does this mean—what is its wider significance?*

- *Application: How does this affect us today?*

Don't be afraid of little silences, and don't be afraid of asking (the more con-fident) individuals by name. Pose (the question)—pause (allow them to think)—pounce (ask a individual). It is all right (for you and for them) not to know an answer!

Sometimes you will find yourself moving off at a tangent. Should you let this continue, or bring people back to the study? This will depend on how important the subject is to the group, and to the individuals concerned. The only way you can judge this is by careful listening.

Follow-up

After each study, it is a good idea to spend a short time reflecting on how things went. Were there simple things that you could do better next time? Think about each person in the group. Who did the most talking? Who said nothing? Who was missing? You should be clear as to who has pastoral responsibility for the group. If someone was upset by something, or someone else was insensitive, who will pick this up and when? Also be clear who you are responsible to. Try and meet with them every few weeks, to review how the group is progressing and to pray for members of the group. And don't forget to enjoy your times together!

Resources

Grove booklets are short introductions to specific subjects, and are a good place to start if you need some help:

P 5 The Wisdom to Listen *by Michael Mitton is an introduction to ways of listening to God, listening to others, and listening to the world.*

P 18 What? Me a House Group Leader? *by Patsy Evans is a practical guide that will help you think further about the issues involved in leading your group.*

P 23 Groups: Asking the Right Questions *by John Finney will help you think about what your group is for, and how you spend your time.*

B 3 Translating the Bible *by Dick France gives a brief history of the translation of the Bible into English, and explains why Bible translations differ and which you should read.*

They are available direct from Grove Books Ltd, Ridley Hall Road, Cambridge CB3 9HU. Tel: 01223 464748.

In preparing these studies, I have referred extensively to William Lane's commentary on Mark in the New International Commentary series (published by Eerdmans). But I have also used two very helpful smaller books: *The Message of Mark* by Morna Hooker (Epworth Press, London, 1983); and *Lion Let Loose* by John Sergeant (Paternoster Press, Carlisle, 1988). All three are accessible to the lay person.

1 'The beginning of the gospel...'

Introduction

The first page of a book normally gives the reader some indication as to what the book is about. The same is true of the Gospels: John's Prologue introduces all the main themes of his Gospel; Luke has a carefully penned introduction; and Matthew sets his story in the context of the ancestry of the people of God. But Mark's introduction is not so obvious in the way it sets the agenda for the Gospel. At first sight, he seems to plunge straight into the story proper, without a moment's hesitation.

But if we look more carefully, we see that a number of themes occur with a prominence that is unmatched elsewhere: visions and voices from heaven; the Holy Spirit; and conflict with Satan. These themes do occur again every now and then, but much more subtly. The focus of all these opening events is the person of Jesus: who he is and the significance of what he does.

Exercise

If you had to summarize your own life-story, what would you include as main themes? (You may have had to do this—in an altered form—for a job interview or something similar.) Write down the most important three or four, and share them with one other in the group. Ask each other: to what extent has Jesus affected or shaped each of these themes?

Read Mark 1:1–15 out loud.

Blessing and judgment (vv. 1–3)

Mark is clear from the beginning that the message about Jesus is 'good news' or 'gospel'; the word translated is *euangelion*. We have picked up different parts of this word in English: you can <u>eu</u>logize about something (speak a <u>good</u> word about it); and an <u>angel</u> is a messenger from God. The *euangelion* is simply a good message. Our word 'gospel' comes from Old English meaning 'good spell' or 'good news'. But was Jesus' message all 'good'?

The passages Mark quotes are Malachi 3:1, Exodus 23:20 and Isaiah 40:3. Have a quick look at these and the surrounding verses.

In what context do these verses come: at a time of blessing or a time of judgment?

Malachi 3:1
Exodus 23:20
Isaiah 40:3

To what extent did the coming of Jesus reflect this: did he bring blessing or judgment (look at verses 1, 14 and 15)?

What has your experience of this been in your life as a Christian? In what ways has Jesus Christ been good news to you? In what ways has he brought judgment?

Baptism and repentance (vv. 4–8)

In Matthew 3, Luke 3 and John 1 much more attention is given to the detail of John the Baptist's ministry and message. Why do you think Mark is so brief in contrast?

What is the significance of John's clothing? Have a look at Malachi 4:5 and 2 Kings 1:8; see also Mark 9:11–13, and compare Matthew 11:14.

The two main elements of John's preaching here are 'baptism' and 'repentance'. What do these terms mean to you?

Baptism suggests acceptance by God, or the giving of something to God in commitment. *Repentance* suggests the turning away from something of which God might disapprove. When we became Christians, and as we grow in our faith, what different things have we found God accepting, and from what have we had to turn away?

The people came to John as a whole—it was not just an individual thing. As we look around our society today, what things are there that we believe God is pleased to accept, and what would he call us to repentance about as a nation or local community?

To what is John referring when he talks of baptism 'with [or in] the Holy Spirit'?

Jesus' baptism (vv. 9–11)

Why do you think Jesus was baptized like everyone else? What does this show about him and his ministry?

The events surrounding Jesus' baptism are full of significance taken from Old Testament expectations. You may wish to explore some of these by looking at: Isaiah 64:1 (the heavens torn open); Genesis 1:2 and Genesis 8:8–12 (the dove); Genesis 22:2, 12 and Psalm 2:7 ('You are my beloved son'); Isaiah 42:1 ('with you I am well pleased').

Which of these aspects of Jesus' identity are significant for you in your experience as a Christian? Why?

Testing in the wilderness (vv. 12–15)

Jesus is tested (better translation than 'tempted') by Satan in the desert. In the Old Testament Satan is the 'accuser' (see Job 2:1–2; also Revelation 12:10), and the wilderness/desert is a place of trial—both for God and the people (see stories in Exodus 17 and Psalm 95).

But who is in control in this passage? How did Jesus end up in the wilderness in the first place?

Although the wild beasts at first seem to be a sign of threat, in the light of Isaiah 11:6 and Isaiah 65:25 how do they become an indication that Jesus is fulfilling the destiny of the promised Messiah?

What sort of situations are 'wilderness' experiences for you? What are the 'wild beasts' that make you afraid? In what way could these become a sign that God is at work in your own life?

Response

Are there any insights which you have discovered in this study that might give you greater confidence in similar situations?

Go back to the exercise and note where Jesus has had an effect on the main themes which summarize your life.

Finish by turning some of the things you have learnt together into simple prayers of thanks for what God has done in your life, whether as blessing or judgment, and/or asking for greater confidence in Jesus in situations where you need it.

 **Notes**

2 Mark 1:21–45
'All who were sick…'

Introduction

The passage we are looking at today is constructed as a sample day in Jesus' ministry—a kind of 'day in the life' of Jesus. With the different themes introduced in principle by the prologue, we now see them working out in practice; Jesus is teaching, healing, casting out spirits in turn, one after another, very much in contrast to the religious teachers of the day.

Twin features of this section are represented by the words 'many' and 'immediately'. The Greek for 'many' occurs more frequently in Mark than in the other Gospels—'many' people come to see Jesus, 'many' are healed, 'many' people get to hear of his work. And all this happens 'immediately'. The word translated 'immediately' or 'at once' comes only twelve times elsewhere in the Gospels, but forty-two times in Mark, and nine times in this chapter alone! It is not so much a case of 'lights—camera—action!' as 'baptism—disciples—action!' Jesus' ministry begins at breathtaking speed.

Exercise

It is now becoming popular for organizations to have a 'mission statement'. But have you ever thought about devising one for yourself? In pairs, think together about what your own mission statement might say. Alternatively, you might want to think of a mission statement for your group, or for your church. Share together and give a prize to the most profound—and the most entertaining!

Teaching with authority (vv. 21–28)

In your own experience, what are the signs of someone speaking with authority—what is it about someone that makes them authoritative? What was it that marked Jesus' teaching out as authoritative? What would make the teaching of the Church in the world authoritative? What about our own witness as Christians?

What is the significance of the cry of the man with the unclean spirit, 'What have you to do with us?' Look up Judges 11:12 and 2 Samuel 19:22 for some clues. How does this fulfil what John the Baptist proclaimed about Jesus?

14

Do you think the people in the synagogue have recognized who Jesus is? Who has? For what reasons might Jesus have commanded the spirit to be silent? (We will be thinking about this further in later studies.)

Healing and prayer (vv. 29–39)

Mark's Gospel is full of eyewitness details. Note that the sick were brought 'at sundown', since this was the Sabbath. Perhaps it took a while for the report of Jesus to get around. But more likely, people waited until the end of the Sabbath to bring those not suffering from life-threatening illnesses, so as not to defile the Sabbath (see Jeremiah 17:21f).

Look carefully at the rest of the chapter, from verse 29. Which people are mentioned by name, and whose name is missing? (You will need to compare versions, and pay attention to footnotes in your Bible.) From whose perspective is the account written? How does that affect the story—what is the atmosphere like in this chapter?

The disciples track Jesus down, and tell him how many people are looking for him—as if he didn't know! They seem to be saying: 'We know what you ought to be doing.' But what priorities does Jesus have in this section? What are the disciples' priorities? How do they differ from Jesus'—what are they most concerned about? What does this say about their understanding of Jesus' mission? What does Jesus' goal appear to be?

Private prayer clearly has a high priority for Jesus, even in the midst of a demanding public ministry, and so he goes to a 'deserted place' (v. 35). What is your 'deserted place' where you can have times with God in prayer and study? The word used here is the same as that used in Mark 1:13 for 'wilderness'. Do you find connections between places of difficulty and temptation, and places of peace and prayer?

His public ministry seems equally concerned with healing and with teaching—with bringing people both to wholeness and to understanding. Which has been most important to you so far in your Christian discipleship—growth in understanding, or growth in wholeness? Which do you need most at the moment? What about your local church?

Doubt and certainty (vv. 40–45)

The man with the skin disease approaches Jesus with a mixture of doubt and certainty. Of what does he seem confident, and concerning what does he appear to have doubts? How does this compare with our approach to asking Jesus for things?

What is Jesus' motivation in this healing? How does he express it? Why might this be significant? How can this be a model for the way we express concern to others?

What does Jesus command the man to do first of all? Why might he have said this? What does it say about how Jesus sees his ministry? Do you think we need to offer 'proof' before we can expect others to come to faith?

Jesus gives the man another command, which at first looks rather odd—the command to be silent. We will come across this again later in Mark's Gospel. Why did Jesus tell the man to keep quiet? What effect did the man's disobedience have—how did it disrupt Jesus' ministry? Whose goals and priorities did the man share—Jesus', or the disciples'?

The man's story clearly had a dramatic effect; what do you think the people who responded were looking for from Jesus?

Response

Reflect on your priorities and pressures for the coming week. On your own, make a list of those things that are priorities for you, and next to each one give the reason why it is a priority. Then think: how has what you have studied challenged these priorities and motivations? Are there any changes you would like to make? Are there any changes you can make? Spend a few moments sharing your thoughts with the group if you feel able, and close with silent prayer committing these to God.

 **Notes**

3 Mark 2
'Old cloth and new...'

Introduction

This is the first of two groups of material that relate to controversies between Jesus and the religious teachers of his day; the second group is in 11:27–12:37, a series of incidents set in Jerusalem. Although the beginning of the chapter is linked to Jesus' preaching tour of the previous verses, the links in verses 13, 18 and 23 are of the most general nature. The material here appears to be an example of Mark bringing things together according to theme, rather than because they happened together.

Jesus' conflict with his religious opponents centres around three issues. The first is to do with who can forgive sins. This was closely related to the authority of God, since the religious teachers believed that no one— not even the Messiah—could forgive sins, but God alone. The second issue was to do with who can follow, who can be a disciple. The Pharisees were very careful to keep themselves separate from anyone who compromised their obedience to the Law in any way. The third issue was to do with who can legislate—how disciples should behave. In different ways, all three questions relate to holiness—its source, its scope, and its nature.

Exercise

Confession time! Think of a habit that you have had for a while, that is amusing, unusual or just plain annoying. Write it on a piece of paper, and put all the pieces in a hat. Draw them out, and see if the group can guess which habit belongs to whom. Why are habits so difficult to change? What things or events have helped you change a habit?

Who can forgive? (vv. 1–12)

What can you tell about the friends of the paralytic from their actions? What were their hopes, expectations, feelings? Jesus responds—but to what (v. 5)? Is this a puzzle, or an encouragement? Why?

What is Jesus' initial response to them? Why is this surprising, and why might it be expected?

It is not entirely clear whether Jesus is forgiving the man on his own behalf, or whether he is declaring the man forgiven by God. Notice that he says 'Your sins are forgiven' rather than 'God forgives your sins.' This way of speaking (the 'divine passive') was a customary Jewish way of avoiding using God's name.

Which is it easier to *say*: that the man's sins are forgiven, or that he is healed? Which is it easier to *do*: to forgive him, or to heal him? The fact that the man is healed is a sign that Jesus' words are effective—in other words, a reassurance of his forgiveness. Should we need reassurance that we are forgiven? How might we receive this?

Who can follow? (vv. 13–17)

Mark gives some very clear indicators as to where the action is happening in these early chapters. Look briefly at 1:16, 21, 35; 2:1, 13; 3:1, 7, 13, 19; 4:1; 5:1, 21 to see Jesus' movement between the three centres of action of town, deserted place/mountain, and sea. This adds to the eyewitness feel of following Jesus around in his Galilean ministry.

Jesus' call to Levi echoes his call to the first disciples in chapter 1. What is Levi's response? What does this suggest about the nature of Jesus' message? Have you ever been aware of the urgency of responding to Jesus?

Why is Jesus criticized for mixing with 'sinners'? What would prevent the Pharisees from mixing with these people? Why is Jesus not worried about this (reflect on Jesus' encounter with the paralytic)?

Are there people that we are reluctant to mix with? What are the good reasons for this (see 1 Corinthians 15:33)? What might be bad reasons for this? It is sometimes said that we should accept people as they are. How does Jesus' description of himself as a doctor qualify this? To what extent can we share Jesus' role here?

Who can legislate? (vv. 18–28)

Fasting was commanded in the Old Testament for two reasons. First, it was a sign of repentance and sorrow for sin, especially associated with the annual Day of Atonement—details can be found in Leviticus 16:29–31 and Numbers 29:7–11. But it was also a sign of mourning (see 1 Samuel 31:13) and of prayer in association with repentance (2 Samuel 12:16). In Jesus' day, the Pharisees fasted twice a week as a sign of personal piety (Luke 18:12).

If fasting is associated with sadness, feasting suggests overwhelming joy. According to Jesus, which should mark his disciples—and when? Which is more appropriate for us today? Do you think Christians need to fast nowadays? Why (not)?

Both new cloth and new wineskins have something in common, that the old lack—they change shape with time. Why do you think new wine needs this flexibility? What is the 'new wine' referring to—what is the new situation that requires openness to change? (Remind yourself of 1:15, 27 and 2:12.)

Think about your experience as a Christian over the last few years, and the life of your church. When have you (and your church) been most like the new wineskin, and when most like the old? What has helped you become more like the new? What might help you now?

The disciples were quite at liberty to pluck grain from another's field (Deuteronomy 23:25), but it was interpreted as work (reaping as they plucked, threshing as they rubbed the grain in their hands, winnowing as they blew away the husk, and preparing a meal as they ate) which were forbidden on the Sabbath (see, for example Exodus 34:21).

How does Jesus' example of David and his men challenge the Pharisees' teaching? What is the new relationship between people and regulations? Think of some 'regulations' or disciplines that you have been taught. Which have helped your walk with Christ, and which have hindered? Why?

Response

When God is at work, doing fresh things with us and our fellowship, this new activity often needs a new understanding on our part. This can be threatening, and lead to conflict. Look at Mark 3:6 to see the Pharisees' response.

Spend some moments in quiet, reflecting on the areas in your life where God has been doing (or where you think he wants to do) something new. Pray together for each other in these areas, using the prayer known as 'The Grace' (2 Corinthians 13:14).

 **Notes**

Mark 4:1–25

'He began to teach them...'

Introduction

Mark mentions to us again and again that Jesus was a teacher, though strangely enough he gives us comparatively little of his teaching. Mark contains only six parables compared with twenty-three in Matthew and twenty-nine in Luke. As we saw in the first study, very often the different elements of the narrative are there not simply for their own sake, but to show us something about Jesus and the significance of his ministry. In Mark, we see very vividly the effect of his teaching on the people who hear; often more attention is paid to this than to the content of the teaching.

The parable of the sower is placed with four other parables or sayings, and together they make up the single largest section of teaching in Mark other than Jesus' teaching on the Mount of Olives in chapter 13. The other parables here are also concerned with the growth of the kingdom of God. They all take a similar form, which is that of an expanded simile or comparison. Jesus confidently uses what is obvious in the natural order of things, the world around him, in order to make known what was previously hidden concerning spiritual things, since both have God as their common origin.

Exercise

In the group, think together: what makes a good listener? Think of someone you know who is a good listener. What are the qualities that that make that person a good listener? How do you rate yourself as a listener?

Seed and soils (vv. 3–9, 13–20)

The parable of the sower is so well known that it can be difficult hearing it afresh. What do you think the parable is about, in essence? The sower, the seed, the soils—or what? Bear in mind Jesus' explanation, and also note verse 11.

Palestinian farmers sowed their land before ploughing, rather than the other way around as in modern agriculture. As a result, all ground was potentially arable, no matter what its appearance at the time of sowing—which part was good would not be evident until the seed had grown. If

God is like the farmer, what does that tell us about how he sees us and those around us?

The seed in the parable sat on the hardened surface of the path, which allowed the birds to see it and take it away. Do you think there are ways in which we can become hardened, so that God's word does not sink in? How can we learn to be more open to hear God?

The rocky ground has a thin covering of soil, so that the seeds cannot grow deep roots. What do you think it means to have strong roots, in our Christian life? (Ephesians 3:17 might be of help.) How can we strengthen our roots?

The thorns are a picture of the things that crowd out and distract us from a faithful response to God's message. What are the things that distract you, and crowd your life? How do you feel about them being described as 'thorns'? In what ways are these things preventing you bearing fruit for God?

Listeners and listening (vv. 9–12)

Look at Jesus' challenge in relation to this parable (v. 9). In what different ways has Jesus and his teaching been received in the preceding chapters? (Look at Mark 1:18, 22, 27, 37; 2:6–7, 12, 16, 24; 3:6, 21–22.)

Jesus' challenge to us is to be good listeners. In terms of the parable, what different qualities make up a good listener? Are these different from the qualities you thought of at the beginning?

These are not just personal things, but can apply to us together as the people of God. Try asking these questions of us as a church: in what ways can we together listen to God? Are there things choking God's work among us?

At first, the quotation from Isaiah seems very harsh, apparently consigning certain people to a failure of understanding. But Jesus says that the parable shows how this comes about—in other words, the parable interprets this quotation. According to the parable, for what reasons do people fail to perceive, fail to understand? Are there any other reasons you can think of?

Think of one thing you would like to do this week to be a better listener to God, and share it with the group if you feel able.

23

The mystery of the kingdom (v. 11)

In verse 11, Jesus suggests that the subject of the parable is 'the secret [or *mystery*] of the kingdom of God'. What do you understand by 'the kingdom of God'?

In what sense do you think that it is 'secret', or 'a mystery'? To whom is this secret revealed?

'Jesus interprets the parables to the disciples because he wants to remove their confusion without reducing the mystery.' In what ways has God been removing confusion for you about the way his rule comes about? Is it still mystery?

Sowers and sowing (vv. 3, 14)

This parable is not only about soils; it is also about a sower and sowing. The process of bearing fruit at the end can only start once the sower has taken the initiative to sow.

Who do you think the sower might stand for? What can we tell about the character of the sower from the way he sows?

God asks us to join in with his work of sowing the seed, of sharing with others the good news of who Jesus is, and what he has done for us. Are there any ways in which this parable encourages you to sow?

Think of one thing you would like to do this week to be a better sower with God, and share it with the group if you feel able.

Response

In the Lord's Prayer, we pray for God's kingdom to come. You may wish, in the group or privately, to use the parable of the sower as a basis for this prayer. For instance, you may pray first for God to break the hardness of heart of yourself or others; for him to help pull up the thorns that prevent growth; and so on.

 **Notes**

5 Mark 5
In action against hostile forces

Introduction

From the very beginning of Mark we have seen that Jesus is in conflict with forces that oppose God. Mark is an 'action' Gospel, and in this chapter we look at three instances of that action. These three stories are unusual in that Mark tells them much more fully than either Matthew or Luke. Numerous points of detail are not included by the other two: the man's cutting of himself and crying out (v. 5), the number of pigs in the herd (v. 13); the financial plight of the woman (v. 26); the comment on how she felt (v. 29); and the details of Jesus' action (in v. 40).

Mark often seems to put his stories together in order to bring out a theme, or to pose a contrast. Here, Jesus is involved with three very different people in very different circumstances: the outcast demoniac; the respectable official; the hard-done-by woman. But his ministry is equally effective in all three cases; in each case the person receives what they want, or need—liberation from the situation they have been in. Notice also the occurrence of fear in each episode: the fear of the people in the first; the reassurance against fear in the second; and the fear of the woman in the third. Mark mentions fear in the context of Jesus' ministry more than any other Gospel.

Exercise

Take a piece of paper, and on it draw a large circle. Draw a horizontal line across the middle of circle and page. The circle is to represent your life, with the upper half your 'outer' life—relationships, activities, work and leisure—and the lower half your 'inner' life—thoughts, anxieties, joys, fears, ambitions, affections. Spend five minutes marking on the most significant people, things and concerns in your life, placing those that you are most comfortable with near the centre of the circle, and those you are least comfortable with nearer the edge. You need not share this with anyone else.

Encounter... (vv. 1–5)

Read verses 1 to 20.

To help you get into the story, you may want to close your eyes as it is read, and imagine what it might have been like to have been there yourself.

Jesus meets a man 'with an unclean spirit' (v. 2). The story is very dramatic; spend a few minutes simply sharing your impressions of what strikes you as significant. What might it have felt like to have been there, witnessing the events?

Notice that the man lived among the tombs. Unlike modern graveyards, these would be well away from the city, and might be caves used as burial chambers where only the very poorest, or outcasts such as this man, might live. Superstition about the dead made this sort of area a kind of 'spiritual rubbish dump'.

What was the effect of the spirit on the man—his relationships with others, his attitude to himself? Scripture tells us that each is made in the image of God; how is this image being destroyed?

There are many things in the world today that crush people and make them less than the human beings God intended them to be—they destroy the image of God in people. Can you think of some of these forces at work in our country and the world? How might we respond to them?

... And response (vv. 6–20)

What is the man's reaction to Jesus? And what impression does Jesus give during this encounter? What does this tell us about his authority? How does this affect your response to destructive forces? Are there areas in your life where you need the reassurance of Jesus' authority?

What is the reaction of the local people? Why do you think that they ask Jesus to go? Are you surprised that he complies with their request? Have you ever felt scared at something that God has done in your life?

The man who has been healed asks to 'be with him', which probably means he wanted to travel with Jesus as a disciple (see 3:14, where Jesus chooses twelve to 'be with him'). Why do you think Jesus refuses his request? Note that his command is different from his command to others who have experienced healing, in one important respect (see for instance 5:43; 7:36; 8:26).

Have you ever experienced the same thing, where you have asked to do something you thought was good and right, and God told you to do something else? How did you come to terms with it?

The good, the bad and the unclean (vv. 21–34)

Read verses 21 to 34; Jesus meets two contrasting people.

Jesus lived in a very religious society. What did that mean for the woman (look at Leviticus 15:25ff)? How does this account for her behaviour? How does she contrast with the other character, Jairus?

Jesus had many people pressing all around him, yet he noticed this woman. What was the difference between the woman and the crowd? In what way is this different from Jesus having 'magical' power? (Glance ahead to 6:6 to help a little more.)

Jesus was prepared to identify with and have compassion on the respectable, as well as the outcast, the 'unclean'. What sort of people in our own society feel welcome in church, and what sort unwelcome? Which groups do we find it easier to relate to? Is there anything we can do to relate to both groups better, after Jesus' example?

The response of faith (vv. 35–43)

Read verses 35 to 43.

The news about Jairus' daughter is bad. What steps does Jesus take in response (vv. 36, 37, 40)? Why do you think he does this?

The common element between the woman and Jairus is faith. In the healing of Jairus' daughter Jesus sends away those who might undermine that faith, that confidence in Jesus which allows him to work. What are some of the circumstances and people who undermine your faith? What are the circumstances that build you up and give you confidence in what God can do?

Response

In these three instances, Jesus goes to areas at the very edge of human experience—possession and lunacy, death, a long-term illness—where those suffering are rejected by others. In each of these situations, fear is present, and is dealt with by Jesus. Think of some of the areas of your life which give rise to fear. What is it you are afraid of? How would Jesus want to remove that fear? You may wish to turn this into personal or shared prayer, perhaps in twos or threes.

 **Notes**

6 'Utterly astounded...'

Introduction

In this study we are looking at two miracle stories that go together—
the feeding of the 5,000 and Jesus walking on the water. The chief
difficulty in trying to understand these is over-familiarity; immediately
they bring to mind stained-glass images of religious occasions. They
seem rather removed from the realities of everyday existence. And at
the same time they seem difficult to 'get inside'; we feel with the
disciples that we have not understood the meaning of the loaves
(v. 52), beyond seeing Jesus as an astonishing wonder-worker.

Mark helps us in this by his continued eyewitness details. The
disciples' exasperation when Jesus suggests they feed the people (v. 37)
is almost tangible. The people sit on the 'green grass', indicating that
this happened early in the year (v. 39). The miracles themselves are
related with Mark's customary simplicity; there is none of the
developed theological significance that we find in John's account. But
these two incidents clearly belong together. If we hold them together,
we may find a way in to understanding them.

Exercise

Have you ever played (or watched) 'What's My Line?' How would you
go about acting out your occupation or a favourite hobby? Try it out,
and see who can guess what it is! Are there any advantages to acting
something out, rather than describing it in words?

Movement and rest (vv. 30–34)

Chronologically, this passage follows on from Jesus' sending out the
Twelve two-by-two in mission (6:7), though in between is an extended
aside about Herod's execution of John the Baptist.

Look at verses 32, 34, 45–46, 53–54. What are Jesus' and the disciples'
movements during this story—what different situations do they put
themselves in? What is the pattern here? How does this compare with
what you know of modern celebrities or 'tele-evangelists'? What insight
does this give into Jesus' motivation in working miracles? What insight
does it give into the needs of Jesus and the disciples?

The disciples have been engaged in a spiritual battle (6:13) and now Jesus
offers them 'rest'. Where else in scripture do we find the pattern of battle
and rest? (See Joshua 1:13–15, and Isaiah 63:14 for a comment on it.)

Jesus' observation that the people are like 'sheep without a shepherd' (v. 34) is also an Old Testament concern. Look at Numbers 27:16–18 and Ezekiel 34:4–6, 23. What are the respective situations, and who will become the shepherd of God's people? How does Jesus respond to the people—what does he see as their chief need?

What does all this tell us about Jesus' ministry? What significance does it give to the miracle that is to follow?

Eating and feeding (vv. 35–44)

Mark nowhere says that Jesus was concerned about the people's physical hunger. Instead, he includes a discussion between Jesus and the disciples that is unique to his account of the miracle (which is recorded in all the other Gospels).

How do you think the disciples felt after returning from their missionary journey (6:7–13, 30)? How were they feeling now, at the end of the day (v. 35)? Who does Jesus want to feed the crowd—where does he say the resources should come from? What effect does this have on the disciples? Why do you think Jesus suggests this?

Have you ever felt as though God has pressed you into a situation where you did not have the resources to cope? Why do you think he did this? How did you respond? What was the end result?

According to Mark's account, who realized that a miracle had taken place? For whose sake did Jesus perform it? What was it supposed to achieve? (See verse 52, and further on to Mark 8:14–21.) How might this affect our understanding of the significance of answered prayer for ourselves?

Lord of the sea (vv. 45–52)

Mark is very careful to point out that Jesus is on his own and the disciples are at a distance from him. How do they react when (really or apparently) abandoned by Jesus? (See 4:35–41 and 9:14–29 for two similar occasions.) It appears as though he is going to 'pass them by'. But this phrase has another significance in the Old Testament: see Exodus 33:19, 22; 1 Kings 19:11. What does this tell us about the meaning of this miracle?

Jesus utters words of assurance that echo God's words of self-revelation in Exodus 3:14, and the assurances found in (for example) Isaiah 41:13 and 43:1. How do the disciples respond? What have they failed to grasp?

Response

Some of the group, or others you know of, may be in situations where they feel they are 'straining at the oars against an adverse wind'. Share with each other about these situations (without breaking confidences of course), and pray quietly while listening to the words of Isaiah 43:1–7 being read out loud.

7 The crucial question

Introduction

The last part of chapter 8 appears to be pivotal in the Gospel. It comes about halfway through, and it marks a shift in emphasis and tone. (You might notice this especially if you read the Gospel through in one sitting; it takes about one hour forty-five minutes to read through out loud, and rather less if you read it to yourself—and is a very worthwhile exercise if you can manage it!) This is the first time that Jesus starts to talk of his own death; he mentions it on two other occasions (9:30–31 and 10:32–34). It also marks the beginning of the journey to Jerusalem; the episode takes place at Caesarea Philippi in the far north of the country, and Jesus and his disciples journey through Galilee for the last time in Mark's account and continue to head south.

There also seems to be a change in emphasis in Jesus' ministry. In the first chapters, Jesus has been teaching the crowds and healing them. From now on, though, his teaching seems much more geared to his own disciples, and rather than healing the crowds, Jesus heals one or two individuals (the boy in chapter 9, and Bartimaeus in chapter 10). Jesus also changes the way he talks about himself, using the enigmatic title 'Son of man'; this occurs only twice in the first half of the Gospel (2:10 and 28), but a dozen times in the second half.

Exercise

Take a few minutes to think of three words that describe the person sitting to your right, and three words to describe yourself. (As you are thinking of the words describing the other person, bear in mind that the person to your left is doing the same for you!) Take it in turns around the room to say how you described the other person, then hear how they described themselves. How do you feel about the description given to you? How does it differ from your description of yourself? Why do these differences arise?

'Who do they say...?' (8:27–28)

Jesus asks the disciples who people think he is. What sort of view do our contemporaries have of Jesus? Where do these ideas come from? What can we do to influence them?

What have the reactions of different people been to Jesus so far in Mark (look back briefly at 1:27; 2:12; 3:6, 21; 5:15; 6:3)? Why do you think they were still confused?

'Messiah' means 'anointed one'. In the Old Testament anointing was a sign of God's appointment of priests (see for instance Exodus 29:7), leaders (1 Samuel 10:1) and prophets (see 1 Kings 19:15–16 and Isaiah 61:1). In Jesus' day, expectations of the Messiah who was to come varied, but they included the expulsion of the Romans (see John 6:15), the establishment of a new kingdom of Israel (Acts 1:6), and the purification of temple worship and sacrifice.

To what extent has he fulfilled their expectations, and in what ways has he not? Like the Jewish people, many Christians find themselves in situations where they long for God to act in a certain way, but find that he does not—or does something rather different. Have you had such an experience? How have you come to terms with it?

Messiah and Son of man (8:29–31, 38)

How does Jesus respond to Peter's confession of him in verse 29? Why do you think Jesus commands the disciples to keep quiet? Are there situations where it is right for us to keep quiet about Jesus?

'Son of man' is also a term that occurs in the Old Testament, and connects two different ideas. First, look at Daniel 7:13–14. In what ways would this image have appealed to the people? Why is this an attractive way to see Jesus? Now have a look at different translations of Ezekiel 2:1, 3:1 4:1 (and so on!). What sort of idea is this communicating—with whom or what is Ezekiel as the 'son of man'/'mortal one'/'human being' contrasted?

According to Mark, what three things does Jesus associate with the title 'Son of man'? You might like to look at the verses in three groups:

2:10, 28; 8:31; 9:31; 10:33

9:9, 12; 10:45; 14:21

8:38; 13:26; 14:62

How might Jesus' use of this term to describe himself help to correct people's wrong expectations of God's Messiah?

In what situations might it encourage us to think of Jesus as a 'Son of man', a person like us, rather than to think of him as 'Lord'? What different things would we share with non-Christian friends if we were thinking of Jesus in this way?

33

Changing perspectives (8:32–37)

In verse 32, Mark comments that Jesus 'said all this quite openly'. Why do you think he makes this observation—who is Jesus talking to? Mark often puts things together to tell us something, and this episode comes directly after the healing of the blind man at Bethsaida. What does Peter have in common with the blind man who is healed, and at what stage of his healing?

Peter—and the crowd—clearly need to change their ideas about Jesus. Jesus talks about 'taking up your cross' daily. In Palestine in the first century, when do you think you would see someone carrying their cross? (When do we see Jesus carrying his cross?)

How does this help us to understand what Jesus means? How might this have helped his disciples and the crowd to understand what Jesus meant when he said, 'You must lose your life'?

In what sort of situations are we ashamed to be identified as Christians? You may want to pray for each other concerning these.

The transfiguration (9:1–8)

The transfiguration points backwards as well as forwards. Compare 9:2 with Exodus 24:9 and 16, and also have a glance at 1 Kings 19:8. What is the significance of the transfiguration in the light of these past events? Why are Moses and Elijah important?

We have heard the verdict of the crowds and the disciples; now someone else gives his verdict! You may want to glance at Genesis 22:2, 12 and Psalm 2:7 to remind yourselves of the significance of the words from heaven.

The crowds do not understand Jesus; the disciples understand something, but have also misunderstood; God knows what he is doing. Have there been times when you have felt misunderstood as a Christian? How have you coped with it?

Response

What three words would you use to describe Jesus, and what he means to you? Think about this for a few minutes, and then share your words with the group, giving reasons if you can. Turn these words and thoughts into short prayers of praise.

 **Notes**

8 'The Lord will come to his temple...'

Introduction

The previous chapters have been building up to Jesus' arrival in Jerusalem—and now he is here. Although Jesus' identity is still only partially seen, for Mark, who knows Jesus' true identity, this episode is full of significance. The Messiah, the one sent by God to rescue his people and open the way for Gentiles to come and worship, comes to the temple, the very heart of Jewish belief and worship. Not surprisingly, therefore, the passage is full of allusions to the Old Testament.

The signs of who Jesus is, in this chapter, are still ambiguous; although the people welcome him rejoicing, these appear to be people who travelled with him, pilgrims, rather than the locals, and their acclaim takes the form of praise to God, rather than a declaration of who Jesus is. The failure of the people, in the form of the religious authorities, to recognize who Jesus is, is set in the wider context of the corruption of temple worship. Their rejection of Jesus was simply the last instance in a long history of failure to honour God and recognize those who spoke in the name of God.

Exercise

Think about some of the ways in which we welcome someone who is important. For example, suppose a national leader came to one of your Sunday services. What would you do to welcome him (or her)? What do these things signify? What things make you feel welcome when visiting a new place?

Of kings and donkeys (vv. 1–11)

Jesus' action in riding on a colt seems to have a significance that the disciples do not notice, and that Mark does not emphasize in his telling. Look at Zechariah 9:9; what features of Jesus' action fulfil Zechariah's expectations? You may also want to glance at Genesis 49:10–11, and see if you can see any connections here.

Why is it significant for Zechariah that the king comes on a donkey? Why is it significant for Jesus? How does this relate to his teaching about why he has come? Does this throw any light on how we should present Jesus to others?

The colt has never been used before. Look quickly at Numbers 19:2, Deuteronomy 21:3 and 1 Samuel 6:7 to see the significance of this. Do you think there is value in having things set aside for God's use alone?

Look at Psalm 118:19–27. What do you see in the psalm that makes it particularly appropriate to be sung as Jesus entered Jerusalem?

Of fig-trees and fruitfulness (vv. 12–19)

Many people find the story of the fig tree difficult to understand. After all, Mark tells us that Jesus could not have expected to find any figs, since it was the wrong time of year. But remember that Mark often puts things together for a reason. Looking at the way the story is told, what do you think this episode is really about? Look at Jeremiah 8:4 and 13 for a further clue.

In what ways is Jesus reflecting Old Testament attitudes to worship and the temple? You may want to get into pairs or small groups and look up some of the following: Isaiah 56:7; Jeremiah 7:8–11; Psalm 69:9; Zechariah 14:20–21; Malachi 3:1–4.

Who is Jesus particularly concerned for, that they should have access to the place of worship (look again at the passage from Isaiah)? What can we learn from Jesus' attitude to worship?

Reflect on your own meetings and services. What sort of people are made to feel welcome? What are the 'requirements for entry' that might put others off? How did you feel when you first came (if you can remember!)?

Of prayer and relationships (vv. 20–25)

What does Jesus set out as the two conditions for effective prayer, in verses 22–25? How do these contrast with the attitude of the religious teachers in Jesus' day? Which of these do you find hardest to live out, and why?

Response

To encourage members of the group, you may wish to spend some time sharing ways in which individuals have seen God answer prayer recently, or perhaps where you have seen answers to prayers you have prayed together as a group. Finish by sharing requests for prayer, so that you can pray for each other during the week. You may like to make a note of these, so you can follow them up in coming weeks.

Mark 14:12–31

The Passover supper

Introduction

Mark has sometimes been described as a Passion narrative (a story about the events leading up to Jesus' trial and execution) with an extended introduction. Although this is something of an exaggeration, the Passion narrative forms the largest single section of Mark's Gospel, and it begins properly with the start of chapter 14. Many of the themes occurring earlier in the Gospel—the conflict with the authorities, Judas' betrayal (first mentioned in Mark 3:19), the certainty of Jesus' death—come into play here. Mark gives a very detailed timetable for everything that happens, and recognition of its reliability helped to shape the early Church's worship; early Easter celebrations tended to follow Mark's timing of events.

Although there is an apparent conflict with parts of John's Gospel, Mark makes it clear that what came to be known as the Last Supper was in fact a Passover meal—the Jewish celebration of God's delivery of his people from slavery in Egypt. This was seen by the Jews as the great act of redemption in history; the word 'redeem', normally used of slaves whose freedom was bought for them, is used in the Old Testament of the Exodus from Egypt, and many hoped that the coming Messiah would similarly redeem his people. The same word is found on the lips of Jesus in Mark 10:45; the 'ransom' of his life is the price paid to redeem many people.

Exercise

You may like to share a simple meal together—and perhaps go through the study whilst at the table, eating a course at a time in between each of the sections.

Preparation (vv. 12–16)

Jerusalem was a small city, perhaps only three-quarters of a square mile in area inside the city walls. Although quite densely populated normally, with a population of somewhere around 40,000, during Passover around a further 120,000 pilgrims came to the city—and all were required to eat the Passover within the city walls! In addition to this would be the 15,000 or more animals to be sacrificed. Spend a few moments, if you can, imagining what it must have been like to be in the city—what would have been the sights and sounds (and smells!) as you walked down one of the narrow streets?

In Jesus' day, men did not carry water jars, but wineskins; only women carried water jars. Therefore, the man carrying a jar (v. 13) must have been a pre-arranged signal. Why do you think Jesus wanted to keep his identity secret leading up to the Passover celebration? (You may want to look at John 11:57 for one answer).

Betrayal (vv. 17–21 and 26–31)

Jesus knows that one of his disciples will betray him (v. 18). Have you ever been let down, or betrayed, by a close friend? Can you describe some of the feelings that you had—or still have—concerning the incident and the person involved? Why does it feel so much worse to be let down by a *close* friend?

In verse 20, Jesus quotes from Psalm 41:9. (The phrase 'dips into the dish with me' signifies sharing bread, sharing a meal—a sign of close friendship.) As you look through the psalm, which feelings can you identify with? Which feelings do you think Jesus identified with at that moment?

Look at verses 27 to 31; the disciples will let Jesus down at the crucial moment. In what situations do you feel you let Jesus down? Remember that you are in good company!

Jesus knows that he will be betrayed—but still offers his life and his love to the disciples. Jesus knows that you will let him down—but still offers his life and his love to you. How do you feel about that? How does it affect the way you think about those situations?

Provision (vv. 22–25)

What do you think 'bread' signifies; what does bread do?

Jesus describes himself as bread (v. 22)—sustaining, giving life, a staple element of diet. (Although he says 'this is my body'—and we are used to hearing these words in the context of communion—the phrase simply means 'this is me, my life'.) In what ways have you experienced Jesus sustaining you? In what situations do you need to claim the promise of Jesus' sustenance and strength?

Nowadays, 'blood' tends to make us think about death (you may want to spend a few moments thinking about why this is). In the Bible, it means the opposite (see, for instance, Genesis 9:4, Leviticus 17:14 or Deuteronomy 12:23). What do you think is the connection between Jesus' offer of his life to us, and his suffering and death?

In the Passover meal, there were four cups of wine passed round; these corresponded to remembering the four things God did in setting Israel free from Egypt (see Exodus 6:6–7), and looked forward to them happening again through the Messiah. What were those four things? From the timing within the meal, we know that Jesus makes his comments over the third cup. What did this one stand for? How does Jesus then see his death?

Commitment (v. 25)

Jesus makes a solemn vow to be committed to God's work of extending his kingdom—similar to the 'Nazirite' vow of commitment to God (Numbers 6:1–4) the same vow binding Samson (Judges 13:7). Why do you think he needed to express this so strongly?

By refusing the fourth cup, which symbolized the completion of God's work in making his people his own (Exodus 6:7), Jesus was committing himself to obedience to God in death, and only after this would he enjoy seeing God's work completed. When will this be? What commitment(s) do you need to make for the extension of the kingdom of God?

Response

You may want to take some of the thoughts provoked by the study into prayer: the questions on betrayal might lead you to prayer of confession, and then of thanksgiving for God's love for us; the last question may lead you into prayer of commitment and dedication. You may wish to pass a Bible around, allowing each member, when the Bible is passed to them, to say a short, simple prayer, silent or out loud as they feel able, before passing the Bible on to the next person.

 **Notes**

10 Mark 15:1–39
The crucifixion

Introduction

We come this week to the climax of Mark's Gospel—Jesus' death. All through the Gospel this has been foreshadowed. The account is full, compared with other events in Mark, though the details of Jesus' two trials, and the crucifixion itself, are quite abbreviated; Mark includes the essentials. There has been much scholarly discussion about the historical details, but it is clear that the important elements accord exactly with what we know from other sources of trials and executions happening at around this time.

The trial (vv. 1–15)

On what charge has Jesus been convicted by the Jewish authorities? (Look back to 14:64.) On what grounds did they find him guilty? (Check back to 14:62, and compare it with Psalm 110:1 and Daniel 7:13.) On what charge is he brought before Pilate? Why do you think the charge has changed?

What do you think Pilate makes of Jesus—does he think Jesus is guilty of wanting to start an insurrection against the Romans? How does Pilate feel toward the Jewish authorities?

How does Jesus behave during his trial—what impression do you get of him? Why do you think he behaves like this? In the light of Jesus' own comments about the nature of his Messiahship (see study 7), why is it significant that he is to be crucified on the charge of claiming to be the Messiah/King of the Jews?

You may want to read Isaiah 53 either now or later on in the study as a reflection on the significance of Jesus' death.

The humiliation (vv. 16–24)

It appears that the account of Jesus' trial was important to the early Christians when they faced discrimination and persecution for their faith. Have you ever been in a situation where you were made fun of, or attacked, for being a Christian? How did you feel about it? How did you cope? Is there anything in Jesus' behaviour that gives you encouragement?

What state would Jesus have been in by now? (Verse 21 might give you a clue.) How did the Roman troops react to him? Inadvertently, they, too, participate in fulfilling the divine plan (see Psalm 22:18).

The crucifixion (vv. 25–39)

How do the passers-by and the priests taunt Jesus? What had Jesus really meant in his prophecy about 'rebuilding the temple in three days'? The priests say they will believe if Jesus shows them proof. What proof do they eventually get? Does that help us when people ask us for 'proof' about God?

What do you think the significance of 'darkness over the land' might be? (Amos 8:9–10 and Exodus 10:21 give some possibilities.)

Why do you think Jesus might have died so quickly? Have a look at Psalm 22 for some remarkable insights into what Jesus might have experienced. Isaiah 53, if you did not look at this earlier, might also give you further insight.

What happened at the moment of Jesus' death (v. 38)? Why is this significant? Why is the soldier's comment important to Mark's readers?

Response

To end this study, sing together or read the words of 'When I survey the wondrous cross', or perhaps 'My song is love unknown'. Alternatively, you might like to read again Isaiah 53 as a meditation.

11 Mark 16:1–8
The resurrection

Introduction

Mark is both odd and unique in lacking an account of the resurrection—peculiar in every sense of the word! In the most reliable manuscripts, the text of Mark ends at 16:8, and others note that the endings we do have did not belong to the original. What we are left with is the empty tomb, the angel's testimony that Jesus had risen, and the women running away in terror and amazement.

But the early Church felt they could not leave it there. The endings that have been added are quite brief, but they sum up something of their beliefs and their experience of living in the light of the resurrection—in the light of meeting with the risen Jesus. The challenge, then, is for us to write our own endings. In what ways have we met with Jesus as we have read Mark's Gospel? How has our understanding grown, and what have we experienced? How will we go about completing the story in our own lives?

Exercise

Share in the group: do you like surprises, or not? What experiences have you had of being surprised—by a surprise party, unusual happening, or perhaps turn of events? Has this been a good experience or bad? Why?

Surprising witnesses (vv. 1–8)

The first people to the tomb were three women, hoping to anoint the body two days after Jesus' death. In the climate of Palestine, they would already have been too late—the body should have been anointed immediately to stop decomposition. But who are these women, and why is it not surprising that they want to see the body? (Look back to 15:40–41.) Why was it important that it was they who were the first there (see 15:47)?

For such a momentous event—foundational in the life of the Church—it was important that there were reliable witnesses. Why is it surprising that the first witnesses of the evidence of the resurrection were women? What problems would this have caused? In what way did this challenge the values of the day?

In your community or church, what kind of people are recognized as having something of importance to say—who is listened to and taken notice of? Whose voice is rarely heard? How does God's 'choice' of witnesses challenge this?

A surprising event (vv. 3–5)

'It reads like an eyewitness's account, not like the dramatization of a religious conviction' (C.E.B. Cranfield). Look through the passage, and pick out the details that point to this being an eyewitness account, that lend authenticity. What is it, precisely, that the women are witnesses to—the resurrection itself, or something else?

Why do they need the comment of the angel ('young man')? Do we need similar commentary on events in our lives? If so, where might we find this?

What does all this teach us about sharing with others our own story of what God has done?

A surprising response (vv. 6–8)

The title 'Jesus of Nazareth' only occurs two or three times elsewhere in Mark (1:24, 10:47 and see also 14:67). Why does the angel make the connection between the risen Jesus and his earlier ministry? Why has Jesus promised to meet them back in Galilee, rather than in Jerusalem (see 14:28)? Why does Peter receive special mention?

What is the women's response to all this—what do they do? Why? Have you ever responded in a similar way to something God has done?

A surprising ending (review)

The women clearly did not keep quiet for long—eventually they overcame their fear and told the other disciples what had happened, so that they could go and see for themselves.

(Study 1) In the first session, we noted that Jesus' ministry promised both blessing and judgment (see Mark 1:1–3). What have you learnt about Jesus' ministry from these studies—in what ways did it bring blessing, and in what ways did it bring judgment? Which have you learnt more about in your own life during these weeks?

(Studies 2 and 4) As Jesus' ministry unfolded, his concern for people involved both teaching and healing (see Mark 2:12–13). What was Jesus' motive for this ministry? How did this differ from those both of the people he ministered to, and of his disciples? How has your desire for Jesus' teaching and healing changed over the last few weeks? What can you do to experience more of Jesus' teaching and healing?

(Studies 3, 5 and 6) Jesus' miracles, healings, and especially the exorcisms, demonstrated his power over unruly forces. Where have you experienced Jesus' power in your life during these studies? Are there areas where you need to experience more of that power?

(Study 7) Jesus allowed others to call him 'Messiah', but described himself as 'Son of man' (see Mark 8:27–31). The disciples took some time to realize who Jesus really was. How has your understanding of Jesus changed as you have studied Mark? How has this affected the way you pray, worship, and go about your daily life?

(Studies 8, 9 and 10) Jesus' entry into Jerusalem, his vulnerability at the Last Supper, and his self-giving in the crucifixion all went against the expectations of the world around him. In what areas of your life do you find it easy to conform to the expectations of those around you—and in what areas are you able to resist these pressures? How have these areas changed as you have read Mark? In which areas do you need to learn more of Jesus' humility and commitment to God's purposes?

Is there something God is calling you to give up for him? Is there something God is calling you to take up for him?

Response

If you were to write your own ending to Mark's Gospel, what would you include? You may want to share ideas in the group; alternatively, you may want to go away and write (say) 300 words of your own—your testimony of what it has meant to meet with the risen Jesus.

 **Notes**

1 'The beginning of the gospel...'

Mark 1:1–15

Aims

• To understand some of the main themes in Mark's Gospel, as set out in chapter 1.

• To reflect on the impact of the good news of Jesus in our lives.

• To grow in confidence in Jesus when we are in difficult situations or periods of our life.

Exercise

This exercise not only helps to 'warm things up' for the study, but is also a helpful way for group members to get to know a little about each other, especially if they have not met as a group before. You will need paper and pencils.

Reading

For ease of reading, break the passage into two halves: verses 1–8 and 9–15. Ask for volunteers to read out loud, or make arrangements beforehand if you do not have confident readers—but always make it clear when you ask someone to read that you agreed this with them beforehand. When it comes to looking up the Old Testament passages, be wary of spending too long on the mechanics of this. If group members do not feel confident finding their way around the Old Testament, note that there is nothing wrong with using the 'Contents' page—that is what it is there for! You can save time by split-ting into three sub-groups, and report-ing back what each group has found to the rest after a few minutes.

Verse-by-verse

1.   The good news is for both Jews—who are looking for the Messiah, the anointed one ('Christ' in Greek)—and Gentiles—for whom Jesus is the Son of God. This twin identification of Jesus is picked up at two crucial points later in the Gospel: at 8:29 Peter declares Jesus is 'the Christ'; and at 15:39 the centurion at the cross recognizes Jesus as 'the Son of God'.

2.   Mark is actually quoting Malachi 3:1, but this verse itself cites Exodus 23:20; the Hebrew '*malach*', translated 'angel', also means 'messenger'; the book of *Malachi* is literally the book of 'my messenger'.

Note also that Mark says that these verses come from Isaiah; you may have noticed in your Bible's footnotes that 'other ancient authorities read *in the prophets*'. These are generally later manu-scripts, which suggests that scribes copying out Mark noticed the mistake and, embar-rassed by it, tried to correct it.

4.   'To baptize' in Greek (*baptizo*) meant to immerse, or plunge, or overwhelm something, usually with water. It was sometimes used to describe the sinking of ships. Baptism was required of converts to Judaism, as a rite of cleansing, and so came to be used for Jewish repentance move-ments in a similar way.

'Repentance', *metanoia*, means a change of mind or attitude. We get our word 'nous' from a similar word. The emphasis is not so much on a feeling of remorse, but on a change of life and action.

6.   The clothing recalls the prophet Elijah, and his return was believed to be the sign that the kingdom of God was coming on 'the great and terrible Day of the Lord'. For many Jews, this meant the judgment

48

of unfaithful Jews and Gentiles, and also the restoration of the nation of Israel to be the true people of God. For many, this also included the overthrow of the Roman Empire. This kingdom would be brought in by the Messiah, ('Anointed One'), once 'Elijah' had prepared the way. But other Old Testament prophecies also point to an expectation that many Gentiles would also come to believe in and obey God.

8.   John's reference to baptism in the Holy Spirit is looking forward to Pentecost and the post-resurrection experience of the disciples. See 1 Corinthians 12:13 to see who is baptized with the Spirit. In the light of the meaning of the word, as being overwhelmed, some members of the group may want to ask questions about their own experience. Note from 1 Corinthians 12 and Romans 6 that Paul sees this baptism as a once-only thing, and that he does not distinguish between water baptism and Spirit baptism very clearly. But this is another whole subject!

10–11.   The text from Isaiah 42 again relates to Old Testament expectations of God acting dramatically in 'the end times' as he had of old. There was a widespread conviction that the Spirit of God had been active and present among his people in the past, that he would come again in the future (Joel 2:28), but that at the moment he was not present. The coming of the Spirit on Jesus marks the beginning of the new age, the coming of the kingdom, the beginning of the end times. See Acts 10:38 for Peter's perspective on this according to Luke.

The significance of the dove is unclear. If it is to do with a new creation (the Rabbis talked of the Spirit hovering 'like a dove' in Genesis 1:2), then this connects with Paul's understanding of new creation in 2 Corinthians 5:17 and Romans 8.

In the past some Christians have held that Jesus only became God's Son at this anointing. But this is difficult to sustain in the light of the birth narratives, and Paul's view of Jesus' pre-existence in Philippians 2:5ff and Colossians 1:15ff.

The other Old Testament references pick up the ideas of Jesus as a sacrifice provided by God (Genesis 22), anointed king (Psalm 2), and suffering servant (Isaiah 42).

Prayer/response

If your group is not used to praying aloud together, a safe way is to pass a Bible from person to person. Whoever has hold of the Bible prays, silently or out loud, before passing it on. This way, there is no anxiety about two people starting at the same time, and each person has space to use in whatever way is comfortable.

2 Mark 1:21–45
'All who were sick...'

Aims

• To think about Jesus' priorities and goals in his ministry.

• To reflect on our own motivations and priorities in the light of this.

• To begin to discover what Jesus' priorities for us in our discipleship might be.

Exercise

Depending on how well your group members know one another, you may want to take this exercise fairly light-heartedly. Mission statements should be short, one-sentence statements of the aim of a group or an individual's life. Thinking about the concept on its own can be quite challenging.

Reading

To retain the impression of non-stop action, you might want to read this passage at one time, though again it is probably best to use different people to read the three sections. If possible, ask people to read who have a fairly literal translation—NIV, RSV or NRSV.

Verse-by-verse

21. When a visitor came to a synagogue, especially if he was someone well-known, or who was 'in the news', it would not be unusual for the local congregation to invite him to teach—probably commenting on the reading from the scriptures, as in Luke 4. It is intriguing that we are not told about the content of Jesus' teaching here, but have to wait until Mark 4 for a sample—and even then, it is a scant sample!

22. Here he teaches as 'one who had authority'; in verse 27 he is one who teaches 'with authority'. The key point here is that what he says is reinforced by what he does. His teaching is not theoretical, but has clear effects. He lives out the reality he proclaims!

23–28. Notice how Mark interweaves the incident of his teaching with the casting out of the demon, in such a way that each episode illuminates the other. We will come across this again on a larger scale in chapters 5 and 11.

24. The phrase 'What have you to do with me?' (or vice versa) is a way of responding to a threat from an enemy, prior to combat. A modern equivalent might be along the lines of 'What's your problem?' or some other threatening challenge!

It would be most common to identify someone as the son of their father (as in 1:19), though not unusual to identify

them by a characteristic (as in 3:17). Jesus' title might suggest that Joseph was no longer alive, supported by the comments in 3:31–32 and 6:3. In Jesus' day, Nazareth was a small town dwarfed by the nearby local capital Sepphoris.

29f. If you read carefully, you will see that Jesus is not mentioned by name in this section, but referred to simply as 'he'. (Most versions have put his name in, often with a footnote, so you can work out who is doing what. More 'literal' translations are more careful about letting you know what the text actually says.) The healing of a member of Simon's family is mentioned specifically, even though it adds nothing in particular to the impression that Jesus cured anyone and everyone. Further, in v. 36 the disciples are referred to as 'Simon and his companions'. These observations support the idea that Mark used Simon Peter's eyewitness testimony as a basis for the Gospel. It gives the reader the feeling of almost looking over Jesus' shoulder, with Simon Peter, in the midst of all the action.

33. It might sound over-dramatic to claim that the 'whole city was gathered around the door'. But Capernaum was a small town, and the population was spread fairly evenly across the countryside. Capernaum and its neighbourhood would probably have had a population of around 15,000.

34. Once again, the use of the word 'many'. It is a Semitic way of speaking, and really means 'the masses' or simply 'everyone'. The Greek word here, *pollus*, has in fact come over into English usage; 'the many' are, literally, *hoi polloi*. In other words, Jesus healed anyone and everyone. Note the same usage later in the Gospel, in 10:45, 'the Son of man came to serve and give his life as a ransom for many'— that is, for the whole world, for everyone.

40. Matthew and Luke both recount this story, but in slightly different contexts, and in less detail than Mark. Though there are

minor variations, all three agree exactly on the words of the man's request, and Jesus' actions and words in reply.

41. Apart from putting himself at risk of infection, by touching the man Jesus was making himself ritually unclean. But he was also tangibly ending the isolation brought about by the man's condition. His comment is particularly terse and dramatic; in Greek it consists of only two words.

43. The details of the sacrifice to be offered can be found in Leviticus 14:2–20.

45. The most obvious effect of the man's disobedience was the practical hindrance of Jesus' ministry. But the many people who came to see Jesus after hearing this man's story may well have been looking for a miracle cure for their ills. We saw earlier that Jesus' ministry had a two-fold aim: healing *and* teaching. He was now prevented from going to the synagogue, the most natural place to exercise his teaching ministry.

Prayer/response

How far you ask people to share their thoughts will depend on how comfortable the group is together. You may wish to end the session by bringing some of the things expressed into a final prayer.

3 Mark 2
'Old cloth and new...'

Aims

• To understand the reasons behind Jesus' conflict with the religious authorities.

• To recognize the need to grow in understanding in the light of what God is doing.

• To begin to face areas in our own lives where God might be challenging us to grow and change.

Exercise

You will need to prepare beforehand some slips of paper, pens and a 'hat' (container of some sort).

Reading

Since we are looking at a whole chapter (albeit a shorter one) it might be easiest to read this in sections, as you come to each group of questions.

Verse-by-verse

4. Mark's accounts suggests that the men dug through the earth of a flat roof. Such roofs were used for drying food, and would have had access by a stairway along one of the walls of the house. Luke's account (Luke 5:19) suggests the roof was tiled. Both kinds of roof could be found in the area. Matthew, interestingly, abbreviates the story and does not mention the hole in the roof (Matthew 9:1–8).

5. There is no need here to assume that the man's paralysis was due to some particular sin, or that somehow Jesus' declaration of forgiveness had a psychological effect that led to the man's healing naturally. There is, however, a general link made in the Old Testament between sin and healing, and the terms are often used closely together (see, for instance, Psalm 41:4, Jeremiah 3:22 and Hosea 14:4).

10. There is an abrupt change in who Jesus is speaking to in the middle of verse 10, and this is present in all three synoptic Gospels. It is common for the accounts of events to differ slightly from one Gospel to

another—but they all tend to converge again when reporting Jesus' words.

13. It does appear that Jesus often leaves the town (Capernaum) and withdraws to the sea after some demonstration of God's power through healing or deliverance. I cannot see any clear pattern of activity associated with each place, though the sea does appear to be closely related to the disciples and their teaching (in 1:16, 2:13 and 4:1 for instance).

14. Tax collectors were universally resented and despised. Levi was probably collecting customs duties, as Capernaum was the first important town on trade routes coming from the north and east through Galilee. Under Roman rule, the right to collect taxes was sold by auction, so the tax collector would make a greater profit the more tax he levied. Tax collectors were disqualified from being judges or witnesses in court, were excommunicated from the synagogue, and their families were held in disgrace.

15. Note that 'many' followed Jesus—a suggestion that the ordinary people, the 'riff-raff' (or *hoi polloi*) were amongst his followers.

16. The Pharisees were careful not to be contaminated by contact with those who did not observe the law as they understood it. But Jesus appears to contaminate others with his holiness, forgiving the paralytic, and accepting the tax collector who then became his follower (presumably with the kind of change of heart shown by Zacchaeus in Luke 19).

21–22. Most people will be familiar with the concept of cloth shrinking. What will be less familiar is the idea of putting wine into wineskins. These are made of leather, which dries out and hardens with use. New wine is still fermenting, and therefore needs the flexibility of a new skin which will stretch with the growing pressure.

26. The incident is related in 1 Samuel 21:1–6—though Abiathar was not then high priest. It was in fact Ahimilech. But the reference may simply be a way of referring to the section in the scroll of 1 Samuel, as Jesus does in a similar way in Mark 12:26 ('in the story of the bush'). Remember that in Jesus' day they had neither books (only scrolls) nor chapters and verses!

28. We will be thinking more about the term 'Son of man' in a later study. The two occurrences in this chapter are the only times Jesus claims the title until chapter 8, after which it is found on his lips frequently.

Prayer/response

In relation to 3:6, it is worth remembering the relation between the Pharisees and Herodians. The Pharisees were the (lay) leaders of a popular 'holiness' movement, who stood against the political compromises of the aristocratic priestly party, the Sadducees. Herod the Great, on the other hand, was a secular ruler, and ruthless and pragmatic when it came to maintaining control. He ordered the temple rebuilt as a show of personal prestige, and as a move to keep the different religious factions happy. One of his sons, Herod Antipas, ruled Galilee at the time of Jesus, with support from Rome. A powerful force indeed was needed to unite the Pharisees with the Herodians!

'The grace of our Lord Jesus Christ, and the love of God, and the fellowship of the Holy Spirit be with us all, ever more. Amen.' If people do not know this prayer by heart, it is worth learning.

4 'He began to teach them...'

Mark 4:1-25

Aims

• To understand the importance of this parable as a key to Jesus' teaching method.

• To reflect on our own listening to God, and think of ways to grow as listeners.

• To grow in our prayer that God's kingdom may come.

Exercise

You may want to get one of the group members to make a note of the qualities of a good listener—or you may want to ask the group at the end what they could remember of what was said, to see how well they were listening to each other!

Reading

You will need to read the parable and its explanation together, but it may be worth leaving verses 21–25 and only reading them if you have time to think about them in this session.

Verse-by-verse

1. 'Again' he taught by the sea—referring back to 1:21 (teaching in the synagogue) and 2:13. But note this is the first real block of teaching material in Mark. You may be able to find a picture in a Bible atlas of 'Sower's Bay' where Jesus supposedly taught this parable. There are certainly a number of bays on the north-western shore of Galilee where this could have happened, and where the shore rises up to form a natural auditorium.

2. Note that Mark does not pretend to be exhaustive—Jesus taught 'many things' in parables, and we have only the pick of the crop.

4–7. It was not uncommon for farmers in Palestine to sow the seed first, and plough the ground afterwards, as opposed to the other way round, as in modern agriculture. The ground would become a packed-down path along the route that passers-by used to cross the field, though this ground would be ploughed up once the seed was sown. There were no public rights of way!

This insight also helps us with the other soils. 'Rocky ground' does not refer to earth with stones in it, but to where the underlying limestone is thinly covered with topsoil; this does not become evident until after the soil is ploughed. Again, it is not clear where the thorns will grow; only when the seed and thorns grow up together does this become obvious.

9. In case you were wondering, the pun in English on ears (of corn, ears to hear) does not work in Greek (the language Mark writes in) or Aramaic (which Jesus may have been speaking in)!

10. Notice that there is a clear differentiation between those on the 'inside' and those on the 'outside'.

11. Jesus' language of secrecy (about the kingdom) forms part of a prominent theme in Mark. Remember that he has commanded silence about himself and his work before (1:43–44 and 3:12) and will do so again (see 8:30). The reason here appears to be theological rather than practical, yet would have the practical effect of sorting out those in the 'outside' who were really interested in understanding from those simply wanting the benefits of his ministry of healing and deliverance.

5 Mark 5
In action against hostile forces

Aims

• To recognize Jesus' indifference to social and religious differences, and allow that to challenge our behaviour.

• To begin to realize that Jesus has authority to act even in the areas at the edges of our experience and comfort.

• To identify ways in which our confidence in him can be developed.

Exercise

You will need paper and pencils or pens for everyone. If possible, try to provide enough space for each person to do this without being overlooked, and make it clear that no one will be expected to share the contents of their 'drawing'. If the connection has not already been made by the group, point them back to this exercise during the response in prayer at the end.

Reading

With its three contrasting characters, Mark 5 is probably best read in sections as you come to each set of questions.

Verse-by-verse

1. The incident happened at a place called 'the Gerasenes'. Although there is some confusion as to its exact location, it probably is the place known as Koursi, on the north-eastern side of Lake Galilee. About a mile south of Koursi there is a steep slope forty yards from the shore, and a further two miles on are cavern tombs which appear to have been used as dwellings at some point. This area is outside Israel proper, and so the inhabitants would be mostly Gentile.

1–8. Notice that Mark is so concerned to communicate vividly, that the order of events gets a little confused. In verse 2 he sums up the encounter; then he gives us some background about the man in verses 3–5; then the man's reaction to seeing Jesus (v. 6); then in verse 7 he tells us what the man is crying out, and goes back in verse 8 to explain what it is that Jesus has said to provoke this.

5. A small note: the text says 'night and day' where we might more naturally say 'day and night'. This is because the Jewish day was counted as starting and ending at dusk, rather than at dawn. The 'mountains' in this region we would call hills.

9. In Jesus' day a lot of store was put by someone's name; it was generally believed that if you knew someone's true name, then that gave you power over them. This may be part of the background to Revelation 2:17 (the gift of a white stone with a name known only to the believer). You might compare the man's reaction with the response of the man in Mark 1:24.

12. It is not clear exactly what the fate of the spirits is once the pigs have drowned, but it appears they avoided final judgment, which Jesus has deferred to a later date. However, their intent to destroy their host becomes plain.

15. Clearly the villagers will have been upset at the financial loss. But at least as great will have been the sense that their orderly view of the world was now upset. The evil man is not as irredeemably evil as they had thought—which perhaps implies that they were not as good as they had supposed. Popular categorizing of people into stereotypes is not a new invention!

19. The undoing of the work of the unclean spirits is to be complete; now that the cause of the broken relationships is dealt with, the relationships themselves must be repaired, as the man returns to his friends and family. Note that, outside the bounds of Israel, there is no injunction to be silent.

22. Jairus' name is probably derived from a Hebrew word meaning 'He will enlighten'; his job title in Mark shows that he was probably responsible for overseeing the arrangement for Saturday services in the synagogue (the local Jewish 'church'), and was a member of the group of either three or seven men who were in charge of that worshipping community. So he is a respectable religious leader and member of the community, though probably a layman.

26. The details of the woman's financial plight resulting from her illness is unique to Mark, as is the comment in verse 29 of her sense of her own healing.

28. Matthew and Luke have her touching 'the fringe of his garment', suggesting that Jesus wore a rabbi's tasselled cloak.

32. 'Jesus looked around' is another eye-witness detail unique to Mark.

40, 43. Again, the observation that Jesus took Peter, James and John and the girl's parents with him is unique to Mark, as is the touching pastoral concern that the girl would be hungry. Jesus was concerned for the whole person!

Prayer/response

With some of the personal things that people may have written during the opening exercise, you might want to allow a time of silent prayer, finishing with a short prayer drawing together some of the thoughts from the group about people on the margins of society, and issues at the edges of our lives.

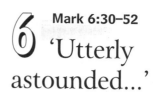

6 Mark 6:30–52
'Utterly astounded...'

Aims

• To understand the significance of Jesus' miracles in Mark's Gospel.

• To see how these miracles fit into the unfolding picture of the identity of Jesus.

• To learn to see God's involvement in the world as teaching us more about him.

Exercise

It might be fun to ask one of the group beforehand to act out something they have done (or do as a hobby) that other members of the group will not know about. See how easily they can guess what the activity is! Alternatively, you could ask for volunteers to act out a task or role that you have chosen beforehand and written down.

Reading

The three sections are very much part of a whole. It is probably best therefore to read them all at once, but ask for three different readers.

Verse-by-verse

30. The disciples get into a 'holy huddle' around Jesus—the verse somehow conveys their excitement at all that has happened during their time out on mission.

31. The reference to a 'deserted place' picks up the theme we explored in studies

1 and 2, though here there is not the overtone of conflict and temptation, only rest. All these echo the Old Testament understandings of the desert, as the place both of hardship and blessing, mainly arising from the forty years' wandering led by Moses. The idea of 'entering rest' occurs throughout the Old Testament; other references include: Deuteronomy 3:20, 12:9f, 25:19; Joshua 21:44; Psalm 95:7–11; Jeremiah 31:2. This theme is picked up explicitly in Hebrews 3:7—4:13. The 'rest' enjoyed by the nation after entering the Promised Land under Joshua becomes a foreshadowing of the all-embracing 'rest' that will be brought about by the Messiah.

Note that 'Joshua' in Hebrew is 'Jesus' in Greek, and that the first Christians would most likely have read the Old Testament in Greek.

33. The crowds recognized 'them', that is, the disciples, and followed *them*. Having been out on mission, the disciples are suffering the pressures of being well-known that up to now only Jesus had faced (in 1:45, 2:1, 3:7 and so on, the crowd follow *him*). That they were unable to eat has been noted before in 3:20. Mealtimes were not just about eating, but about relaxation and fellowship as well.

37–38. Many people will think of John's account, where the loaves and fishes belong to a small boy. But in Mark, the thrust of this dialogue is that the disciples themselves are to provide for the needs of the crowd—something they clearly feel unable to do. Can you detect the note of desperation in their rhetorical question (v. 37)?

44. Unusually for one of Jesus' miraculous acts, Mark records no response from the crowd. In other words, the miracle has been for the benefit of the disciples—Jesus performed it not to impress the people, but to help his followers understand who he was. As with Jesus' commandment of secrecy to those he had healed earlier in the Gospel, and his explanation of parables only to the 'insiders', the disciples have been given privileged access to the truth about Jesus—but still have not understood (v. 52).

46. Again, Jesus retreats up a mountain after a display of God's power, as we saw in 1:35, 3:13 and elsewhere.

48. The phrase 'pass by' is used of God's glory in the Old Testament passages; you may have to ask those with more literal translations to read their version to allow you clearly to see the parallel to this verse.

50. In the Greek text, the phrase 'It is I' is the same as the phrase in the Greek version of Exodus 3:14 for 'I AM', God's self-designation to Moses.

Prayer/response

Allow some minutes for people to share the situations they are in, or know of—but keep focused on the fact that the aim of this sharing is so that you can pray together! You may want to read the passage aloud (slowly, after some silence) yourself, or arrange beforehand for someone else to read it.

7 Mark 8:27—9:13
The crucial question

Aims

• To understand the significance of the terms 'Messiah' and 'Son of man'.

• To recognize Jesus' challenge to the expectations of his followers then and now.

- To begin to think through the implications of Jesus as Son of man.

Exercise

You will need to give each person a pencil and paper for this exercise. Keep an eye out to make sure that no one takes it *too* seriously, and take note if any get upset about another's description of them!

Reading

You may want to read this in sections again. It may be worth leaving chapter 9, and only read it if you have time to answer the questions on the transfiguration.

Verse-by-verse

8:30. Why does Jesus command silence? This touches on the discussion of the hiddenness of Jesus' message in earlier studies. Part of the answer lies in Jesus wanting to provoke people into asking questions and finding out more, part lies in the fact that Jesus looks for a response of faith, rather than proof, and part lies in the danger of the people misunderstanding his role as Messiah.

8:31. There is some debate amongst scholars as to the exact significance of the term 'Son of man'. It started life as an Aramaic expression by which the speaker referred to himself in slightly self-effacing terms, and to this extent it emphasizes Jesus' humanity. (Aramaic was one of the languages spoken in Palestine, and was similar to Hebrew.) Many of the occurrences in Mark are in the context of Jesus' referring to his death. But it also gained significance from Daniel 7:13, and some of Jesus' sayings refer back to this. It seems as though it was a useful way for Jesus to avoid misunderstandings that arose from the term

'Messiah', and to talk about his identification with humanity, his suffering and death, and at the same time his future vindication by God through the resurrection.

Note that the phrase 'son of man' in Ezekiel is translated variously as 'Mortal', 'Human', 'O Man'; in Daniel 7:13 it is sometimes translated 'one looking like a human', or similar. It is up to you how far you go in discussing the term. You will need to find a couple of different translations amongst members of your group in order to make sense of the references in Ezekiel and Daniel. You can use the looking up of references to split the group into pairs, or get individuals to do a bit of 'research' and then report back to the group.

The three groups of verses relate roughly to three kinds of sayings of Jesus—the first group (2:10, 28; 8:31; 9:31; 10:33) to predictions of the passion, the second group (9:9, 12; 10:45; 14:21) to Jesus' own death and suffering, and the third group (8:38; 13:26; 14:62) to his coming on the clouds in glory. But note that this division is approximate, and there is overlap. Split your group into three, and ask each to look at one set of verses. The net result of this is that Jesus' victory was to come through suffering, rather than instead of it.

Once we have grasped the significance of Jesus the Son of man there is much appeal in seeing him as 'one of us'. Many find it an encouragement to know that Jesus went through the sorts of things that we do, the frustrations and irritations as well as the joys of life, rather than seeing him as some superhuman figure who never had any problems.

8:33. 'Get behind me!' is less a command to get out of the way than a call to follow Jesus as a disciple. The same word ('behind/ after') is used both here and in the next verse ('If anyone would follow after me...'), though this is obscured by most English translations.

9:4. Moses was the Law-giver, and the Law was of central importance to Judaism. Elijah was the prophet *par excellence*. In addition, the Old Testament was known as 'the Law and the Prophets', so that to some extent Moses and Elijah between them sum up God's revelation of himself to Israel.

Prayer/response

Again, it is good if each person writes these words down. Encourage short, simple prayers of thanks, based on what you have discussed.

⑧ Mark 11:1–25
'The Lord will come to his temple...'

Aims

• To understand the significance of Jesus' entrance into Jerusalem.

• To think about the connection between worship and prayer (on the one hand) and our attitude to others (on the other).

• To discover ways in which our public worship and our relationships need to grow and develop.

Reading

As there are a number of different issues in this section, it may be worth reading each section separately, rather than reading the whole passage in one sweep. This way, you have some space

and a marker before you move on to the next section.

Verse-by-verse

1. You may want to look at a map in the back of a Bible (or in a Bible atlas) to see where these incidents happen. Jesus and his disciples have apparently travelled down the Jordan valley, and climbed up through Jericho to arrive at Jerusalem from the east. Although this does not look like a very direct route, the central area is very hilly, and observant Jews would probably want to avoid travelling through Samaria. The route from Jericho up to Jerusalem— though dangerous—was a popular route for pilgrims.

2–3. Note that there may be nothing mysterious about the procuring of the donkey; Jesus nowhere else in Mark refers to himself as 'the Lord', so his comment in verse 3 may simply mean 'Its lord [i.e. owner, perhaps a follower of Jesus] needs it.'
    The points brought out in Zechariah are that the king comes to Jerusalem (to rescue her); the people rejoice to see the king; and he comes riding on a donkey rather than a war-horse. God's coming is humble, and in marked contrast to the power of the forces from which he rescues his people. This is in line with the theme of Zechariah: 'Not by might, nor by power, but by my spirit, says the Lord of hosts'(Zechariah 4:6, NRSV).
    Genesis 49:10–11 is difficult to understand, though it was thought to be some sort of prophecy about the coming of the Messiah. Verse 10 in some versions mentions 'he who comes'; some think that there is also significance in the tying and untying of the colt.

9–10. Psalms 113–118 were known as the 'Hallel' psalms; 'hallel' means 'praise', and these psalms were sung in the temple during Passover, probably a week away if we follow

Mark's timetable of events in this section. Apart from the use of Psalm 118 in temple worship at this time of year, there are several elements in the psalm of relevance: v. 19 talks of entering the temple to worship; v. 22 is used elsewhere in the New Testament of Jesus (Luke 20:17; Acts 4:11; 1 Peter 2:7) and sums up his rejection by the Jewish authorities; in v. 24 the people rejoice; v. 27 mentions the use of branches in procession.

'Hosanna' comes from the Hebrew (*hoshiah-na*) meaning 'Save [us] now' (see Psalm 118:25). 'Jesus' is the Greek form of 'Joshua' (*ye-hoshua*), which is from the same Hebrew verb and means 'God saves' or 'God is salvation'.

13. Since the leaves are on the tree, it is probably spring, which agrees with Mark's setting of the incident near the time of Passover. Fig trees do have green, bitter figs before the leaves come, but these fall off so the tree has only leaves. The edible figs grow later in the year.

The story of the fig tree is a sort of living parable concerning the worship of the people. In the Old Testament the fig tree is a picture of God's people (as is the vineyard, see Mark 12, the following chapter). God finding good figs stands for the people worshipping in the right way, and living according to God's commands. The barren fig tree is a sign that things have gone wrong, and that judgment is to come.

15. It appears that the introduction of traders into the temple area was a recent innovation in Jesus' time. There was already provision for the changing of money (in order to pay the temple tax) and purchasing of animals for sacrifice in the form of four markets on the Mount of Olives, less than a mile from the temple.

The markets in the temple precincts would have been sited in the Court of the Gentiles, thus effectively excluding Gentiles from the only area in which they were allowed, in order that Jews would more easily be able to offer sacrifice. See if anyone in your group has a diagram of the temple area in the back of his or her Bible.

17. Mark's story seems to be alluding quite clearly to the Old Testament passages mentioned. The passage in Jeremiah 7 accuses the people of looking for security in the building of the temple, rather than an actual relationship with God, or perhaps even in nationalist zealot (armed) forces (the 'robbers'). This last point might be of relevance, given that when the Romans destroyed the Jerusalem in AD70, the temple was the last stronghold of the Jewish fighters to fall.

We can learn from Jesus not only in his attitude to worship, but also perhaps from the fact that he takes the Old Testament (the only scriptures he had) seriously!

22–25. The two conditions are: believing that God will act; and forgiving our neighbour. These two themes of trust in God alone and openness to others are an exact contrast to the religious leaders, who are concerned to appease Rome, and not bothered about excluding Gentiles from access to the temple.

Prayer/response

It can be encouraging for group members if the group keeps a 'prayer diary' where requests are noted down, and space is left to note answers to prayer and encouragement. This not only helps the group to thank God, so that prayer is not simply a 'shopping list' of requests, but can also help to build faith in God who answers prayer. You may like to appoint a prayer 'scribe' to keep this book up to date.

Mark 14:12–31

9 The Passover supper

Aims

• To understand some of the background to the Last Supper, and thereby grasp more of its significance.

• To identify patterns of experience that reflect the dynamics of the events, and so make connections between the text and life.

• To renew commitment to action to see God's kingdom extended.

Exercise/visual aid

Whether or not you share a meal together, it would be a great help to the group if you are able to have a loaf of bread on display in the middle of the group, together with four glasses or goblets, the third of which should contain red wine. You may also want to buy some *matzos* (Jewish unleavened bread, available in most supermarkets) to display alongside the loaf. It is probably similar to the bread Jesus broke, though has different associations in our culture.

Reading

The passage is quite long; you may want to break it up and ask several people to read—though it is worth reading right through at the beginning of the study, rather than reading section by section with the questions.

In discussing questions about 'betrayal' and 'provision', some members of your group may share personal, painful experiences, and even recent experiences that still hurt. These need to be handled with care; be careful not to move on too quickly, or offer glib answers. You may feel it is appropriate to pause in your study, and pray for a particular person, if they are happy for that to happen. Alternatively, you may prefer to discuss these questions in twos or threes, before coming back together again.

In looking at Psalm 41, some may find it expresses their feelings well, and may identify with the parts which call for vengeance. If this is so, try and make sure the group avoids condemning such identification; this might prevent honest sharing in the future.

Verse-by-verse

12. Try and encourage the group to imagine a little of what it must have been like in Jerusalem at this time. It would be useful if any members of the group have been to Jerusalem, or to a similar Middle-Eastern city, and can share some of their impressions. There must have been a lot of bustle and noise and confusion! It may be worth thinking about the *smells* of the city too!

13. Thinking about Jerusalem at Passover shows that it was *possible* for Jesus to stay anonymous; remember too that in the days before the mass media, people would not know what Jesus looked like unless they had seen him. There may have been several reasons (remember the 'secrecy' motif, as well as the threat of the authorities) why it was *necessary* for Jesus to stay hidden—and therefore why it was necessary for the authorities to have one of his companions lead them to Jesus.

60

14. There is no need to suppose that Jesus had miraculous knowledge here. We know that he had friends (Martha, Mary and Lazarus) who lived near Jerusalem, and that it would therefore have been possible to make these arrangements as anyone else would.

17. Note that, as before, Mark tells us the time of day.

20. You may notice as you look through that near the end of the psalm is a comment that God will 'raise up' the psalmist. Jesus may well have interpreted this for himself as God's promise of resurrection—especially as he uses the phrase in v. 28.

23. The four things in Exodus 6:6–7 corresponding to the four cups are: God will bring his people out; he will free them from slavery; he will redeem them; and he will make them into his own people.

24. The question of exactly why Jesus has to die to allow us to be forgiven, and have new relationship with God, is obviously an enormous area for discussion! You may want to use this question as an opportunity for members simply to share their own understandings of why Jesus' death is important. If the group really is in a fog, then you may want to come back to this subject at a later date; the discussion may serve simply to highlight that group members need to think about this further.

Prayer/response

As well as time in prayer, you may also want to spend some time looking at Isaiah 53, which many read as a foretelling of the events of Jesus' death. Alternatively, there are several songs that set the words of Isaiah 53 to music, for example, 'He was pierced for our transgressions' by Maggi Dawn (*Songs and Hymns of Fellowship*, 173).

10 Mark 15:1–39
The crucifixion

Aims

This is a more reflective study, and the aim is as much for people to be moved by the account of the crucifixion as for them to understand more about it.

Exercise

You may like to begin this study with a time of quiet, or sing an appropriate song together.

Reading

This is quite a long passage, but it is very much of a piece. Ask someone who is a confident reader to read each section as you come to it; breaking it up will make it manageable, whilst having the same reader provides continuity.

Verse-by-verse

1. In Roman subject territories, as Judea was in Jesus' time, much of the local administration and the power of local leaders was left intact—even the power to find someone guilty of a capital offence. The one power that the Romans always retained was the execution of capital punishment. So once the Jewish authorities had found Jesus guilty, they had to ask Pilate to execute the sentence.

Note the time that the Jewish leaders come to Pilate. This agrees with what we know of Roman practice: cases were always tried immediately it was light, and the officials would have leisure time later in the day.

2. Roman trials would always happen in public, and Pilate probably based himself at Herod's palace, in the west end of Jerusalem. The normal format for a Roman trial was that an official would state the charges, and then the magistrate (in this case, Pilate) would listen first to the witnesses, and then the defendant, before passing judgment.

9. Pilate does not want to fulfil the wishes of the Jewish leaders, and tries to find a way out by consulting the crowd—but it backfires. This ties in with what we know of Pilate from other sources; according to Philo and Josephus he despised the Jews, and often seemed to go out of his way to upset them.

15. There are two significant points in this part of the passage that echo parts of Isaiah 53. Isaiah 53:7 makes a point about the silence of the Servant, and 53:6 and 12 are echoed here in verse 15. In the version of the Bible that Christians would have read, Isaiah 53:6 says that God 'handed him over to our sins'; verse 12 says '... because he was handed over to death', and Mark 15:15 says that Pilate 'handed him over to be crucified'.

16. Jesus has just been flogged; Roman whips used for this had sharp pieces of bone twisted into the cords, so that they tore the flesh during the flogging. It was not uncommon for men to die of this alone.

Note that the 'whole battalion' (v. 16, RSV) come to make fun of him. This might have been anywhere between 300 and 600 men. Clearly Jesus had caused quite a sensation.

21. Men going to be crucified usually carried the cross-beam themselves, but evidently Jesus was too weak to do this. It may be that Simon of Cyrene's sons were known in the early Church in Rome; a Rufus is mentioned in Romans 16:13.

37. Crucifixion was well known to be an extremely cruel and painful death, though it was common, being the normal Roman punishment for insurrectionists. Those crucified sometimes lasted for up to three days; death was slow and by suffocation, dehydration and exhaustion. The centurion supervising Jesus' execution is surprised at the speed and manner of Jesus' death.

38. The tearing of the curtain in the temple is, apparently, well-attested in Christian and non-Christian sources.

39. The centurion's comment about Jesus would not have had the religious meaning that it has for us, but, ironically, would have had political overtones, in that the Emperor was known as 'Son of the gods'. Remember, too, that Mark's audience was probably Roman.

11 Mark 16:1–8
The resurrection

Aims

• To (re)discover the surprise of Jesus' resurrection.

• To review the lessons learnt from the studies, and reaffirm ways in which what we have learnt has made a difference in our daily lives.

• To think again about areas where we need to grow and move on.

Exercise

This can be quite revealing—you may be surprised at who does not like surprises!

Reading

This short passage should be read as a whole.

Verse-by-verse

1. Mark 15:40 makes it clear that the 'Mary mother of Joses' in 15:47 and 'Mary mother of James' in 16:1 are in fact the same person. It is not clear why her title changes from one verse to the other, unless the sections were written at a different time, or designed to be read at different times. Although the women have not featured in Mark's account of Jesus' ministry, the comment in Mark 15:41 ties in with the fuller statement in Luke 8:1–3.

As the ones who had seen where Jesus' body was laid, it is highly unlikely that they would have mistaken the tomb for another.

In Jesus' day, women were not regarded as reliable witnesses, and were not allowed to take a full part in religious practice. Contemporary religious teachings and prayers include comments such as: 'Sooner let the words of the Law be burnt than delivered to women'; 'Happy is he whose children are male, and alas for him whose children are female'; 'Blessed art thou, O Lord God, king of the universe, who hast not made me a woman.' (All these are cited by C.E.B. Cranfield in his commentary on Mark, page 464.)

2–5. Mark appears to be precise about the time the women went to the tomb, though there appears to be a slight discrepancy with the other Gospels. They have a very natural concern about the stone (we are told that it is very large) but in the emotion of the moment have not planned ahead how they might move it. The tomb itself would probably have consisted of a low entrance into a room cut into the rock, around seven feet square and the same height, with benches cut into each wall for bodies to be laid out on. We are told that the angel is sitting 'on the right' for no good reason. All these add to the sense of an eyewitness account.

We know the young man is some sort of heavenly being, because white is the colour of heaven (see Mark 9:3 for another example of 'unearthly' whiteness).

6. Note the connection here with 15:47—the place where they laid him.

8. The verse ends with the women being afraid, and the final phrase in Greek has a slightly unusual word order. This had led some to speculate that the subsequent verses were lost, but recently a number of scholars have shown that a similar order of words occurs elsewhere in endings in ancient literature. This makes it more likely that Mark simply did not write anything beyond verse 8—for whatever reason.

Note

You may wish to be selective in your use of the questions reviewing points raised in previous studies—especially if you omitted one or more of studies 2, 3, 4, 5 or 6.

Prayer/response

If your group is confident, you may like to encourage them to turn their shared testimonies into short prayers of thanksgiving. If the group is not confident praying aloud, use the method explained in the first session, passing a Bible around the group. You may like to finish by singing an appropriate song, such as 'Thine be the glory' (*Songs and Hymns of Fellowship*, 545) or 'I live, I live, because he is risen' (*Songs and Hymns of Fellowship*, 202).

Text copyright © Ian Paul 1996

The author asserts the moral right to be
identified as the author of this work.

Published by
The Bible Reading Fellowship
Peter's Way, Sandy Lane West
Oxford OX4 5HG
ISBN 0 7459 3508 7

First edition 1997
10 9 8 7 6 5 4 3 2 1 0

Acknowledgments
Unless otherwise stated, scripture quotations are
taken from the New Revised Standard Version of the
Bible copyright © 1989 by the Division of Christian
Education of the National Council of the Churches
of Christ in USA.

Scripture quotations marked (RSV) are taken from
the Revised Standard Version of the Bible copyright
© 1946, 1952, 1971 by the Division of Christian
Education of the National Council of the Churches
of Christ in USA.

A catalogue record for this book is
available from the British Library.

Printed and bound in Malta
by Interprint Limited